Believe in Yourself Therapy

written by
Daniel Grippo

illustrated by
R.W. Alley

**ONE
CARING
PLACE**
Abbey Press

Text © 2005 by Daniel Grippo
Illustrations © 2005 by St. Meinrad Archabbey
Published by One Caring Place
Abbey Press
St. Meinrad, Indiana 47577

Library of Congress Catalog Number
2005936472

ISBN 978-0-87029-397-9

Printed in the United States of America

Believe-in-yourself Therapy

Foreword

Sometimes, life throws us for a loop. Whether it be the death of a loved one, a serious illness or injury, the loss of a home or job or cherished relationship—setbacks and losses come to us all. At these times, we may begin to doubt our own abilities or judgment, and our self-confidence and self-esteem may plummet. We may feel lost, confused, or empty inside.

This little book of gentle meditations offers hope, encouragement, and some simple steps you or a loved one can take to begin restoring your self-confidence and self-trust. The truth is, you already possess all you need in order to heal, to adapt, and to grow in confidence. You simply need to reconnect to the goodness and the possibilities within and all around you.

This book is designed to help you move forward with renewed self-confidence, wiser and stronger, as you once again embrace life with purpose and joy. Believe in yourself, and all else will follow!

1.

Do you remember, as a child, how everything seemed possible? When we played, we ran with the wind, we built castles in the sky, we were masters of the universe!

2.

All the doors of life were wide
open when we were young.
We could be doctors, athletes,
firefighters, saints, astronauts,
maybe even president! Our
parents said, "Work hard and
the world will be yours."

3.

It is good that we dream dreams. They help us grow and stretch and find our way in the world. And it is important that we start life with a healthy belief in our own abilities and goodness.

4.

As we mature, however, setbacks and losses come our way. We realize that we're not all-powerful, and things don't always go our way. Things happen that we can't change, and we make mistakes that we can't easily fix.

5.

The death of someone we love
is a life experience, for certain,
that changes our perception
dramatically. We can't bring
our loved one back, and we
may be unsure of who we are,
and what we should do,
without them in our life.

6.

The bre...
relatio...
feeli...
mo...

...ak-up of a close ...nship can leave us ...g adrift, torn from our ...orings. Alone on the sea ...f life, we feel buffeted by the shifting winds. We've lost our rudder, and we're not sure where we're headed.

7.

Serious illness deeply challenges our sense of who we are. What has happened to our strength, our energy, our ability to act in the world? Feeling weak and having to depend on others is difficult when we're used to taking care of ourselves.

8.

The loss of a job, a career failure, a serious economic setback—even retirement, if we're not prepared for it—can shake our self-confidence. We may feel unwanted, even useless. Our self-esteem can plummet.

9.

When someone we love very much and feel responsible for, such as our child, goes astray in life, we may be haunted by questions such as, "Where did I go wrong?" "What should I have done differently?"

10.

A long-distance move cuts us off from all that was familiar. We may feel alone and unsure of ourselves in our new environment. Who are we now, and where do we belong?

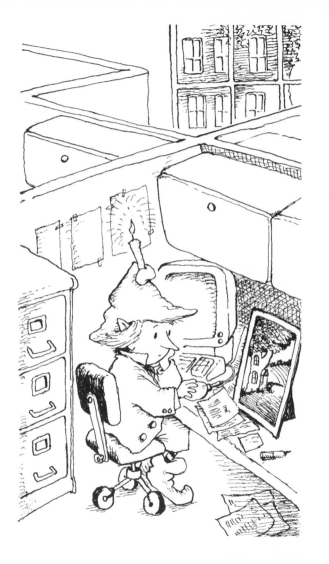

11.

When we make a serious
mistake or hurt someone
we love through selfish or
thoughtless action, doubt
and shame may overcome us.
Our self-criticism only adds
to the downward spiral in
our self-esteem.

12.

If we feel betrayed by someone or something we long believed in, our value system is shaken to the core. It's hard to know exactly who or what to trust anymore.

13.

Life does indeed have some difficult lessons for us. We learn that our dreams don't always come true, and we don't always live up to standards—someone else's, but more often, our own.

14.

Our sense of who we are has been battered. How do we believe in ourselves in the face of unexpected changes, losses, hardships? How do we trust our own judgment and abilities in uncertain times?

15.

When life knocks us for a loop, we need to rebuild a healthy sense of self-worth and self-confidence. The good news is, there are practical steps we can take to restore them. And we can start today.

16.

Self-forgiveness is an important first step. Forgive yourself for being human, for making mistakes. It's okay if you sometimes feel weak, confused, or just plain unsure of yourself. It's part of the human condition.

17.

Forgiving ourselves helps us accept ourselves. We may not like every aspect of who we are or the situation we're in, but constructive change comes more naturally if we start by accepting what is.

18.

When it comes to building or rebuilding self-confidence, small steps are best. Think of one simple thing you can do today to make progress. If nothing comes to mind, clean something—your room, your office, the dishes. It's a start, and that's all you need today.

19.

When we start with small tasks that give us a sense of accomplishment, we gain the confidence to tackle bigger ones. Maybe yesterday you cleaned the kitchen, and today you're ready for—the garage! Organizing our surroundings helps us collect our thoughts.

20.

Remember the slogan, "Progress, not perfection." Tack it on a bulletin board or post it on the refrigerator. It reminds us that we can still believe in ourselves even when things go wrong or we lose our way.

21.

A positive attitude can work wonders, regardless of the situation. You may not have done everything perfectly, but you have done your best, or can do so now. Remember, the glass is only half empty if we fail to see that it is also half full.

22.

Positive people affirm us, and make us feel good about ourselves. We need and deserve such people in our lives, especially in difficult times. Seek out those who affirm you. Spend time with them.

23.

Natural beauty lifts our spirits and helps us realize that even if all is not possible, much certainly is. Look around you at the abundant fullness of nature. Your life is also filled with abundant possibilities. You *can* trust life. You *can* believe in yourself!

24.

Regular exercise keeps us physically fit, mentally alert, and emotionally calm. Every day should have its share of physical movement. No need to sprint if that's not your style; a brisk walk will do just fine.

25.

When we look our best, without going to costly extremes to do so, we feel our best. Treat yourself to a new outfit or a haircut.

26.

What and how we eat affects
our mood, our energy, and our
self-image. Avoid mindless
snacking or using food to calm
your nerves. Instead, invite
others to share meals with
you. Make meals a time for
conversation and kindness.

27.

An inspiring book or movie lifts and ennobles our spirits and helps us once again believe in the goodness and possibilities of life. A funny movie or book makes us smile, restoring our sense of well-being.

28.

Spiritual reading and reflection help us find a deeper ground in which to root our self-identity and self-worth. The lives and lessons of the great spiritual teachers help us realize that they, too, faced adversity and doubt. They met the challenge, and so can you!

29.

An active spiritual life helps us believe in our own goodness and gifts. The support of a faith community lifts us up when times are tough. Stay connected and get involved. Helping others reminds us of how much we have to offer.

30.

Hold your fears and doubts up to the clear light of reason. Tease them apart. What are they really made of? Many doubts and fears dissolve and disappear when we realize they are based on nothing more than an overactive imagination.

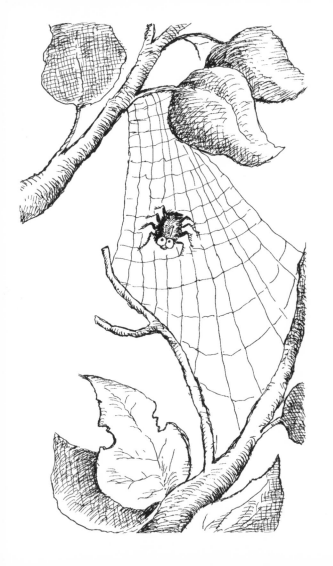

31.

Ask for help when you need it.
When you're feeling down or
isolated, call a trusted loved
one who knows you well.
They understand that you've
been bruised and shaken, and
they will be there to listen.

32.

If you feel stuck, a trained counselor, spiritual guide, or other professional may be able to help. A current setback or loss can trigger memories of older ones, and we may have some earlier damage to repair. Learning to trust ourselves is always a work in progress.

33.

No matter the source of your shaken confidence, you can recover. We can't undo mistakes, but we can learn from them and make amends. We are not perfect, but we are good, and we are trustworthy.

34.

As you focus on rebuilding, embrace new interests and activities that "stretch" you. Maybe you've always wanted to paint, or write, or play the clarinet! Take a class. Attend a workshop. You will gain new confidence when you realize what you are capable of.

35.

Accept a bit of awkwardness as you learn new skills, meet new people, make new beginnings. The awkwardness will soon pass, and the new-found sense of accomplishment will make it well worth the effort. You will surprise yourself!

36.

Be patient with yourself. After a major setback or life change, we need to redefine who we are and where we're heading. That takes time, and there are "growing pains." That's okay—you're moving forward with life, learning to believe in yourself again.

37.

Look for a deeper source of meaning in your life. Prayer and quiet meditation will bring you in contact with that deeper source, and you can turn toward God with confidence. You are worthy, just as you are. You are loved, just as you are.

38.

As you get in touch with Everlasting and Eternal Love, you will realize that you are already complete, just as you are. And you will know with assurance that there is indeed much you can believe in— starting with you, yourself!

Daniel Grippo is an author and co-publisher for TrueQuest Communications of Chicago. He is the author of *Worry Therapy* (20093), *Loneliness Therapy* (20078), and *Healing Thoughts for Troubled Hearts* (20058) in the Elf-help series. He wishes to dedicate this book in loving memory to his mother.

Illustrator for the Abbey Press Elf-help Books, **R.W. Alley** also illustrates and writes children's books. He lives in Barrington, Rhode Island, with his wife, daughter, and son. See a wide variety of his works at: www.rwalley.com.

The Story of the Abbey Press Elves

The engaging figures that populate the Abbey Press "elf-help" line of publications and products first appeared in 1987 on the pages of a small self-help book called *Be-good-to-yourself Therapy*. Shaped by the publishing staff's vision and defined in R.W. Alley's inventive illustrations, they lived out the author's gentle, self-nurturing advice with charm, poignancy, and humor.

Reader response was so enthusiastic that more Elf-help Books were soon under way, a still-growing series that has inspired a line of related gift products.

The especially endearing character featured in the early books—sporting a cap with a mood-changing candle in its peak—has since been joined by a spirited female elf with flowers in her hair.

These two exuberant, sensitive, resourceful, kindhearted, lovable sprites, along with their lively elfin community, reveal what's truly important as they offer messages of joy and wonder, playfulness and co-creation, wholeness and serenity, the miracle of life and the mystery of God's love.

With wisdom and whimsy, these little creatures with long noses demonstrate the elf-help way to a rich and fulfilling life.

Elf-help Books

...adding "a little character" and a lot
of help to self-help reading!

Christmas Therapy (color edition) $5.95   #20175

Happy Birthday Therapy   #20181

Forgiveness Therapy   #20184

Keep-life-simple Therapy   #20185

Acceptance Therapy   #20190

Keeping-up-your-spirits Therapy   #20195

Slow-down Therapy   #20203

One-day-at-a-time Therapy   #20204

Prayer Therapy   #20206

Be-good-to-your-marriage Therapy   #20205

Be-good-to-yourself Therapy   #20255

Book price is $4.95 unless otherwise noted.
Available at your favorite gift shop or bookstore—
or directly from One Caring Place, Abbey Press
Publications, St. Meinrad, IN 47577.
Or call 1-800-325-2511.
www.carenotes.com